Consoling Thoughts
of
St. Francis de Sales

—Fourth Book—

Consoling Thoughts on Eternity

Consoling Thoughts

of

St. Francis de Sales

—Fourth Book—

Consoling Thoughts on Eternity

*Gathered from His Writings,
And Arranged in Order, by the*
Rev. Père Huguet

TRANSLATED FROM THE FRENCH
27TH EDITION

*"You cannot read anything more useful than the works of
St. Francis de Sales, in which everything is pleasing
and consoling."*—Fenelon.

TAN Books
An Imprint of Saint Benedict Press, LLC
Charlotte, North Carolina

TAN Books
An Imprint of Saint Benedict Press, LLC
Charlotte, North Carolina
2013

St. Francis de Sales' Loving Heart

"Through a great part of my soul I am poor and weak, but I have a boundless and almost immutable affection for those who favor me with their friendship. Whoever challenges me in the contest of friendship must be very determined, for I spare no effort. There is no person in the world who has a heart more tender and affectionate towards his friends than I, or one who feels a separation more acutely."
—St. Francis de Sales.

"It has pleased God to make my heart thus. I wish to love this dear neighbor ever so much—ever so much I wish to love him! Oh! When shall we be all melted away in meekness and charity towards our neighbor! I have given him my whole person, my means, my affections, that they may serve him in all his wants."—St. Francis de Sales.

CONTENTS

Publisher's Preface

S T. FRANCIS de Sales was a man of great passion. Reading his thought is to know his heart. Has Holy Mother Church ever reared a child so willing and able to express his longing for perfect union with God? Has a man so learned ever presented Truth and Beauty so simply?

Words cannot fully express the Publisher's appreciation for this Gentle Saint, the Bishop of Geneva and Doctor of the Church. Saint Francis was a lawyer, a theologian, and a missionary. As a young priest, he volunteered to re-evangelize the Calvinist of Chablais, France. He preached not only with conviction, but also with unparalleled gentleness and grace. He worked tirelessly, even under the cover of night, slipping his apologetic writings beneath the doors of anti-Catholics. The Lord rewarded him with one of the most remarkable and well-documented events in Catholic history when nearly the entire population of 72,000 Calvinists returned to the Faith.

This volume, *Consoling Thoughts*, is representative of why St. Francis was so well-received in Chablais, and indeed, throughout history. Perhaps more than any other saint, St. Francis preached truth with love. His teachings, his works, and his very presence were consoling to those 72,000 lost souls of Chablais and to millions of more over the centuries. Now, then, it is our hope that they will offer consolation to a new generation of Catholics.

It is for this reason that TAN Books is proud to bring this compilation of St. Francis' writings back to print. Initially published in a single volume, we now present this work in a four volume series, carefully arranged by topic to give solace in times of darkness, or, simply in times of deep meditation.

It is the Publisher's sincere hope that *Consoling Thoughts* finds a permanent home in your library and among our long list of Saint Francis de Sales classics, including *Introduction to the Devout Life*, *Treatise on the Love of God*, *Catholic Controversies*, and *Sermons of St. Francis de Sales* (in four volumes).

Saint Francis de Sales, Doctor of the Church, *Pray For Us.*

Robert M. Gallagher, Publisher
November 19, 2012

Preface to the Sixth French Edition

By Père Huguet

SIX editions of this little work, published in a short time, tell better than any words of ours the popularity which St. Francis de Sales enjoys amongst us. Many sick and wounded souls have found in these sweet and affecting pages a heavenly consolation.

Encouraged by this success, the honor of which belongs to God and His blessed servant, we have again with pen in hand run through the works of the Bishop of Geneva, to glean carefully whatever had escaped us on our former tour. Nor has our labor been in vain; we have gathered new flowers, whose beauty and perfume yield in no respect to the first.[1] To introduce them in this edition, we have been obliged to lop off a good many of the old chapters which were so well suited to the object of the book. We have acted thus with the less regret as we have published the omitted

---

1 The author has scarcely taken anything from the *Introduction to a Devout Life*, this admirable book being in the hands of everyone.

portions, complete, in two other volumes: the *Consoling Piety of St. Francis de Sales,* and the *Month of Immaculate Mary, by St. Francis de Sales.* These two works form a complete course of consolation for all the trials of life.

We may be permitted to give a short extract from a late number of the *Catholic Bibliography,* which contained an article on *Consoling Thoughts.* The idea of publishing the article was most remote from our mind, on account of the many marks of very great kindness towards us which it bears; but remembering that the merit of this work belongs entirely to St. Francis de Sales, we have felt impelled to give at least an extract, as a new and encouraging proof of the opportuneness of our little book.

"The very title of the book," it says "pleases, and should secure a large number of readers. How many souls are there today who stand in need of being encouraged and consoled? Want of confidence is the great obstacle in the work of the Christian apostleship. Discouragement is the evil of our period, because in general the Christian life, or SANCTITY, appears like a sharp mountain, which only few persons can ascend; in despair of arriving at its summit the majority of men remain below on the plains. The mere word 'sanctity' frightens. The *Lives of the Saints,* which ought to encourage, often discourage, by their list of heroic virtues; we gladly conclude that such a state of perfection is suited only to a very small number, and we remain out of the ways of sanctity for fear of not being able to walk in them.

"Blessed then be the pious author who has received the happy inspiration of assembling together the *Consoling Thoughts of St. Francis de Sales,* the sweetest and most amiable of the saints, and one of the greatest masters of the spiritual life!

"It is especially by his admirable union of firmness and mildness that St. Francis de Sales shines in the first rank of ascetic writers. Who else ever painted virtue under lovelier colors, or made it easier or more practicable? Whoever knew better how to enlighten and bring back souls that had withdrawn from God, or that wearied themselves in His service by an unreasonable fear?

"Happy then and useful inspiration [it was], to gather from his works the thoughts most fitted to enlighten pious and timorous souls, to console them, and to dilate their hearts dried up by fear! Father Huguet has given us, in this little work, the quintessence of everything that our amiable saint wrote most sweet and consoling, especially in his letters, in which that heart so good and tender, which God had formed to comfort the afflicted, is entirely revealed. The book is of the greatest assistance to the simple faithful, and to directors and confessors charged with comforting discouraged and troubled souls.

"A word now as to the method adopted. The author read, he tells us, with pen in hand, the works of the holy Bishop of Geneva; and, after noting the different passages which referred to the same subject, he arranged them in such order as to form a single chapter. A page is thus sometimes collected from seven or eight places in the saint's writings. Yet such is the connection of ideas that we scarcely perceive the labor, and everything seems to flow as from one fountainhead. As to the graceful, artless style of St. Francis de Sales, the author has lightly retouched it in some

xiv   CONSOLING THOUGHTS OF ST. FRANCIS DE SALES

places, changing a few antiquated expressions that would be little intelligible nowadays. Without altering anything in substance, he has considered it a duty to suppress certain details and comparisons, whose want of simplicity, a common fault at present, might cloy the work. Everywhere we have the good shepherd, who, after the example of his Divine Master, instructs, cheers, and consoles, by the help of parables and similitudes, in the great art of using which perhaps he never had an equal.

"To add more clearness and authority to the book, the author has, from time to time, placed at the foot of the page some notes taken from the most esteemed writings of our greatest masters of the spiritual life, particularly Bossuet and Fenelon. These notes, happily selected, give a new value to the work. Should we now recommend it to all those whose souls have need to be encouraged and consoled—in a word, all the faithful?"

INTRODUCTION

By Père Huguet

"The writings of St. Francis de Sales are the fruit of grace and experience."—Fenelon.

THE great evil of our period is discouragement. Tempers and characters have become weak and degenerate. Everyone agrees in saying that the most common obstacle, and the one most difficult to be overcome, which all those meet who labor for the conversion of sinners and the sanctification of pious souls, is want of confidence. The great evil that Jansenism wrought in the midst of us has not yet entirely disappeared: many still believe that perfection consists only in fearing the Lord and in trembling before Him, who, in His mercy, permits us to call Him *Our Father,* and to name Him *the good God.*

The generality of authors have placed in the *Lives of the Saints* an account of their heroic virtues only, without a single word of the defects and miseries which God left in them, in order to preserve them in humility and to make them more indulgent towards their brethren; yet the history of their weaknesses would, according to the judicious remark of St. Francis de Sales, have done the greatest good to a large number of souls, who imagine that sanctity can, and should, be exempt, even in this world, from all alloy and all imperfection. It is to remedy, as far as lies in our power, these inconveniences, that we have gathered together, under appropriate headings, from the writings of the sweetest and most amiable of all the saints, those passages which are best calculated to enlighten pious souls, and to expand their hearts withered with fear.

The writings of St. Francis de Sales are admirably suited to times of trial and sadness. The soul enjoys in them an atmosphere of mild salubrity that strengthens and renews it. The doctrine there is holy and profound, under a most amiable exterior; the style adds, by its simple naïveté, to the charm of a clear and ingenuous fancy; we are instructed while we imagine ourselves distracted, and admire while we smile.

We hesitate not to say that no saint has ever contributed so much as St. Francis de Sales, by his immortal writings, to make piety loved and practiced in all classes of society.

"Under his pen," says the best of his biographers, "devotion is noble, true and rational; courtesy of manners, a spirit of sociality, all the charms of a well-ordered piety, form its cortege, if we may use the expression, and yet it is not disguised in order to appear the more agreeable. Everywhere the author's sweetness appears without weakness, and his firmness without bitterness. He teaches us to respect decorum, which he calls the gracefulness of virtue, to rise above nature without destroying it, to fly little by little towards Heaven like doves when we cannot soar thither like eagles, that is to say, to sanctify ourselves by ordinary means. There the mind contemplates truth, unveiled in majestic splendor, bedecked with maxims equally elegant and profound, clad in a style noble, flowing and natural, relieved by the justness of the expressions, sometimes fine and delicate, sometimes vivid and impressive, always graceful and varied: this is simplicity, with all the merit of beauty, for every idea is rendered by the proper word, and every word embellishes the thought. There, above all, the heart tastes an inexpressible pleasure; because the sweetness of the sentiment always seasons the precept, while the delicacy of the precaution that accompanies it secures its acceptance, and the artless candor and goodness of the author, who paints himself without intending it, make him beloved; at the same time the soul, embalmed in what it reads, deliciously participates in the sweetest and purest perfume of true piety."[1]

The style of St. Francis de Sales is a picture of his heart as much as of his mind: we feel that he loves and deserves to be loved, but that he wishes above all things that we should love God.

A special characteristic of St. Francis de Sales is that the frequent use he makes of figures and the comparisons which he endlessly multiplies, never weary. This style

---

1 *Life of St. Francis de Sales,* by M. the Curé of Saint Sulpice. This beautiful work has met with a success which surprises no one except its author, whose modesty and evangelical simplicity can alone equal his learning and his zeal for the conversion of souls.

would be clumsy in another author; with our saint it is a new pleasure, which draws away the reader and attracts him every moment, as a gentle magnet, and this with so much the more ease as the reader does not perceive it. One is led along unresistingly, yielding with pleasure to the charms of this enchanting style. An effect, so rare and wonderful, is owing not only to our saint's judicious choice of figures and comparisons, but also to his amiable character, to the sprightliness of his sentiments, and to the transports of his love for God, which burst forth even in the midst of the most abstract truths. He cannot contain the fire that consumes him; he allows it to escape by every sense. Moreover, he so well unites simplicity of diction with beauty of metaphor, that, in perusing his works, we feel the ornaments to flow from his pen without an effort on his part to seek them. A tender and compassionate soul, he is full of charity towards his friends. Let us hear him speak: "Through a great part of my soul I am poor and weak, but I have a boundless and almost immutable affection for those who favor me with their friendship. Whoever challenges me in the contest of friendship must be very determined, for I spare no effort. There is no person in the world who has a heart more tender and affectionate towards his friends than I, or one who feels a separation more acutely."

We have so often heard the following affecting words repeated, that they seem to have fallen from the mouth of the sweet Saviour Himself: "It has pleased God to make my heart thus. I wish to love this dear neighbor ever so much—ever so much I wish to love him! Oh, when shall we be all melted away in meekness and charity towards our neighbor! I have given him my whole person, my means, my affections, that they may serve him in all his wants."

This benignity, this gentleness, which breathed through the whole conduct of our saint, made St. Vincent de Paul exclaim with touching simplicity: "O my God! How good must Thou be, since the Bishop of Geneva is so good!"

It is in his works that he deposited the richest treasures of this sweet sensibility and of this playful imagination, which enabled him to lend to the driest subjects and the severest precepts of the evangelic law a charm that makes them loved even by the profane.

The French Academy proposed the writings of St. Francis de Sales as a model to all, even at a time when it extolled the faults of Corneille.

To make himself all to all, St. Francis de Sales descends to the level of the simple faithful, and there he loves to rest. Sometimes he places himself with his *Philothea* in the midst of the stormy sea of the world, and there casts out the anchor of faith; again, he takes his stand on the high road to show to the multitude, who pass indifferent and distracted along, the narrow way that leads to Heaven. We might say that he smoothes its roughness, so carefully does he conceal it under flowers. These are not deceitful flowers, by which virtue is disfigured in the endeavor to render it more attractive; they are those flowers of the soul which perfume without corrupting it, secret joys, interior consolations, ineffable delights, the anticipated inheritance of God's elect upon earth. The picture which he draws of devotion can only be compared to that of charity by

St. Paul. "In his writings," says Père de Tournemine, "we have the morality of the Sacred Scriptures and the Holy Fathers reduced to true principles and practical rules."

The doctrine of St. Francis de Sales is like a beautiful river which takes its rise in pure and elevated regions, and which, descending to the lowlands, spreads wide its banks, in order to reflect a broader expanse of Heaven; it is decked with the flowers of the prairie which it gathers on its course, and carries to the sea a tribute only of limpid and perfumed waters.

According to St. Francis de Sales, we must not be too punctilious in the practice of virtues, but approach them honestly, with liberty, in a *grosso modo* way. "Walk simply in the way of the Lord," he says, "and do not torment your mind. We must hate our defects, but with a tranquil and quiet hatred—not with a spiteful and troubled hatred—and, if necessary, have patience to witness them and to turn them to account by a holy self-abasement. For want of this, my daughter, your imperfections, which you view so closely, trouble you much, and by this means are retained, there being nothing that better preserves our defects than fretfulness and anxiety to remove them." (*Sermon for the Feast of St. Magdalen*).

He applies to himself what he counsels to others: "I know what sort of a being I am; yet even though I feel myself miserable, I am not troubled at it; nay, I am sometimes joyful at it, considering that I am a truly fit object for the mercy of God, to which I continually recommend you."

This devotion, at least in appearance so easy, naturally

pleases persons of the world, who, like the Count Bussy-Rabutin, say: "I merely wish to get into Heaven, and no higher." This nobleman, writing in another place, says: "Save us with our good Francis de Sales; he conducted people to Heaven by beautiful ways." Yet these beautiful ways were no other than the narrow way of which the Gospel speaks; only our amiable saint knew how to smooth its entrance and to hide its thorns under flowers.

St. Francis particularly excelled in comforting the afflicted and the sick; a few words falling from his heart sufficed to calm and enlighten them; his words entered into their soul as an oil of great sweetness, which moderated the heat of their malady. Let us hear him console a pious person to whom sickness was an insupportable burden: "Be not annoyed to remain in bed without meditation, for to endure the scourges of Our Lord is no less a good than to meditate. No, indeed; but it is much better to be on the cross with Jesus Christ, than merely to contemplate Him in prayer." To another, who was troubled at the sight of her miseries, he said: "When we happen to fall, let us cast down our heart before God, to say to Him, in a spirit of confidence and humility, 'Mercy, Lord! For I am weak.' Let us arise in peace, unite again the thread of our affections, and continue our work."

St. Francis de Sales was so much the better qualified to tranquilize and encourage souls inclined to diffidence and depression, as he had himself been obliged to pass through the severest trials, and arrived at the possession of peace of heart only by a total abandonment to God. "Since at every season of life, early or late, in youth or in old age, I can expect my salvation from the pure goodness and mercy of God alone, it is much better to cast myself from this moment into the arms of His clemency than to wait till another time. The greater part of the journey is over; let the Lord do with me according to His will; my fate is in His hands; let Him dispose of me according to His good pleasure."

The pious M. Olier, that great master of the spiritual life, very much esteemed St. Francis de Sales. "God," he says, "wishing to raise him up as a torch in the midst of His Church to enlighten an immense number, replenished him with the most marvelous gifts of understanding, knowledge, and wisdom, proportioned to His designs. As for his knowledge, it was evidently more than human, and the effect of the Divine Spirit."

If you wish to know Francis de Sales thoroughly, to be initiated into the most secret mysteries of that vast understanding and that perfect heart, read and re-read his *Letters,* in which every subject, from the most humble to the most sublime, from a simple how-do-you-do to a description of ecstasies and eternal beatitudes, is treated of in the style that best suits it. Read, above all, the *Letters to Madame de Chantal,* and those which treat of the *direction of souls.* Considering these admirable letters, Bossuet says: "Francis de Sales is truly sublime; there is no one among moderns with such sweetness, who has a hand so steady and experienced as his, to elevate souls to perfection and to detach them from themselves." The letter written after the death of his mother is of a primitive simplicity, and a sublime model of Christian resignation; we imagine that we hear

St. Augustine weeping over St. Monica, and the tears it makes us shed have nothing of bitterness, so sweet is the death of the just when thus related.

The learned and pious Archbishop of Cambray continually recommended the perusal of our saint's writings. "You cannot read anything more useful," says Fenelon, "than the books of St. Francis de Sales; everything there is consoling and pleasing, though he does not say a word but to help us to die. His artless style displays an amiable simplicity, which is above all, the flourishes of the profane writer. You see a man who, with great penetration and a perfect clearness of mind to judge of the reality of things, and to know the human heart, desires only to speak as a good-natured friend, to console, to solace, to enlighten, to perfect his neighbor. No person was better acquainted than he with the highest perfection; but he repeated himself for the little, and never disdained anything, however small. He made himself all to all, not to please all, but to gain all, and to gain them to Jesus Christ, not to himself."

To this judgment of the pious Bishop of Cambray we shall add that of the learned Bourdaloue: "The doctrine of St. Francis de Sales is a food, not of earth, but of Heaven, which, from the same substance, nourishes, like the manna, all kinds of persons; and I am able to say, without offending against the respect which I owe to all other writers, that after the Holy Scriptures there are no works that have better maintained piety among the faithful than those of this holy bishop."

The illustrious Monsignore of Paris shared the same

sentiments. "All that can contribute," he says, "to make the most amiable of saints better known to the world must be useful to the cause of our holy religion."

Thus, the three men who were the glory of the clergy of France in the age of Louis XIV were unanimous in esteeming and praising the works of this great master of the spiritual life.

Protestants themselves are obliged to render justice to the exceptional merit of the works of St. Francis de Sales. One of their best authors[2] thus appreciates the writings of the blessed Bishop of Geneva: "From its first appearance, the *Introduction to a Devout Life* had a universal success in France, and editions succeeded one another rapidly. This was an event of great consequence in regard to such a book, and Catholicism could most justly rejoice at it. The learned controversies of Bellarmine had been of far less advantage: they had indeed fitted for theological discussion a clergy who found themselves face to face with superior forces; but from the first blow, the *Introduction* could make conquests to a religion whose practices were presented under forms so amiable, and even so delightful. . . . Among Calvinistic gentlemen solicited to abjure their faith, the little book served as an occasion for more than one renunciation. In this respect, the *Introduction to a Devout Life* was, in the beginning of the century, what the *Exposition of the Catholic Faith* was in the middle, and had effects quite similar. Of all that St. Francis de Sales has written, his *Letters* are the most widely spread: Protestants read them after a selec-

---

2   *History of French Literature,* by M. Sayous.

tion, for all would not suit their taste; but in each class, the amiable and glowing piety, the grace—what shall I say? the wit, the familiar gossip, with which the Bishop allows his pen to twirl along, have a singular charm; and never does the afflicted or dejected heart disdain the consolation and encouragement which it finds in perusing them."

It is in his correspondence that we must study the great, the holy Bishop of Geneva; there we shall find humility unparalleled, a joyous cordiality, peace unutterable, the sole desire of accomplishing the will of God.

There we shall find that elegance, ever new, in thought and in expression; that richness of beautiful images and of fine comparisons borrowed from things most familiar: the rose, the pigeon, the halcyon, the bee, the odorous plants of Arabia; that dovelike simplicity, that childlike candor which does not, however, exclude, on due occasions, a manly strength and energy; that chaste tenderness which could only come from Heaven; that gentle meekness which holds the key of every heart.

We shall be the less surprised at the eulogies given to the writings of St. Francis de Sales by the most experienced doctors and the most eminent personages, when we consider with what maturity and wisdom they were composed. Those beautiful pages, which seem to flow as from a well, so free and natural are the doctrine and the style, are the fruit of the most serious study and the most assiduous meditation, joined with a great knowledge of the human heart, which he had acquired in the direction of souls.[3]

---

3   *Spirit of St. Francis de Sales.*

His beautiful *Treatise on the Love of God* is the result of twenty-four years' preaching, according to the statement of the author himself, and the fruit of such profound study, that there are fourteen lines in it, which, as he told Mgr. Camus, Bishop of Belley, had cost him the reading of more than twelve hundred pages in folio.[4] After this, we should not be surprised at the unexampled success which has crowned the writings of St. Francis de Sales. The *Treatise on the Love of God* is a most beautiful book, and one that has had a great circulation. All the agitations, all the inconsistencies of the human heart are painted in it with inimitable art. We behold there the exercises of love, contemplation, the repose of the soul in God, its languors, its transports, its dereliction, its dying sadness, its return to courage, the abandonment of the docile spirit to the secret ways of Providence. When the *Introduction to a Devout Life* appeared in the world, it created an extraordinary sensation; everyone wished to procure it, to read it, and, having read it, to read it again. Very soon it was translated into nearly all the languages of Europe, and editions succeeded one another so rapidly that in 1656 it had reached the fortieth. Henry IV, on reading it, declared that the work far surpassed his expectations; Mary of Medici, his wife, sent it bound in diamonds and precious stones to James, King of England; and this monarch, one of the most learned who ever occupied a throne, conceived such an esteem for it, that, notwithstanding his schismatical and spiteful

---

4   It is related that the publisher, in gratitude for the considerable gain he had derived from the sale of the *Introduction to a Devout Life,* made a journey to Annecy expressly to offer as a gift to the author a sum of four hundred crowns of gold. *(Memoirs of the Academic Society of Savoy,* Vol. II).

prejudices against Catholic writers, he carried it always about with him and often read it. Many times he was heard to say: "Oh, how I should wish to know the author! He is certainly a great man, and among all our bishops there is not one capable of writing in this manner, which breathes of Heaven and the angels." The general of the Feuillants, speaking of this work, calls it the most perfect book that mortal hand ever composed, a book that one would always wish to read again after having read it many times, and he adds this beautiful eulogium, that in reading it he who would not be a Christian should become better, and he who would be better should become perfect.[5]

The Church, directed by the Holy Spirit, exhorts all her children to be guided by the counsels of St. Francis de Sales. *Admonished by his directions,* she says in his Office. She assures us that his works have diffused a bright light amongst the faithful, to whom they point out a way as sure as it is easy, to arrive at perfection.

We could, if our design permitted it, multiply evidence in favor of the works of St. Francis de Sales. We shall terminate this introduction by some extracts from a letter of Pope Alexander VII, one of the greatest of his panegyrists: "I conjure you anew to make the works of M. de Sales your delight and your dearest study. I have read them I cannot tell how many times, and I would not dispense myself from reading them again; they never lose the charm of novelty; they always seem to me to say something more than they had said before. If you trust me, these writings should be

---

5 *Life of St. Francis de Sales,* by M. the Abbé Hamon.

xxviii CONSOLING THOUGHTS OF ST. FRANCIS DE SALES

the mirror of your life, and the rule by which to form your every action and your every thought. As for me, I confess to you that from often reading them I have become like a repository of his most beautiful sentiments and the principal points of his doctrine, that I ruminate over them at my leisure, that I taste them, and that I make them, so to speak, pass into my very blood and substance. Such is my opinion of this great saint, exhorting you with all my heart to follow him."

If in gathering these lovely flowers and binding them into bunches, we have lessened their beauty or their perfume, we trust that still they will at least a little serve those severely tried souls for whom we intend them; we shall consider it an ample recompense for all our trouble, if, even in a single heart, they increase confidence in God, and the desire to love and serve Him generously.

"Most holy Mother of God, the most lovable, the most loving, and the most loved, of creatures! Prostrate at thy feet, I dedicate and consecrate to thee this little work of love, in honor of the immense greatness of thy love. O Jesus! To whom could I more fitly offer these words of Thy love than to the most amiable heart of the well-beloved of Thy soul?"[6]

---

6 Dedication of the *Treatise on the Love of God,* by St. Francis de Sales.

—Fourth Book—

Consoling Thoughts on Eternity

CHAPTER ONE

THE CHRISTIAN MANNER IN WHICH WE SHOULD MOURN OVER THOSE WHOM WE HAVE LOST

IF WE lose our parents and friends, we ought not to be too much distressed; for there is no reason in the world why we should desire those whom we love to remain a long time here, and we ought rather to praise God when He takes them away, than be grieved at it. In the same manner we must all, one after another, depart, according to the order which has been established; the first who leave, only find themselves the more fortunate, when they have lived with care of their salvation. And then, in eternity, such losses are repaired, and our society, broken up by death, will be restored. This is a very sufficient consolation for the children of God, when their parents and friends have received the efficacious remedies of the holy Sacraments, before dying; which they ought always to procure without delay.

Let us keep our hearts in repose and without bitterness;

but let us have courage, if there be need, to close the eyes of our dear departed one, giving him the kiss of peace. After which, let us render, without much pomp, the little honors which the Christian custom requires, according to the state and condition of everyone. Especially, let us see that the prayers are said, and other pious exercises performed, exactly according to the intention of the deceased, for fear he may have need of some expiation through the severity of the divine judgment, that he may not be long deprived of the enjoyment of a full and glorious liberty—that his soul may not be imprisoned, through some of God's inscrutable secrets, for a time in Purgatory, before being received into the arms of the divine goodness in Heaven.

By this last journey, friendships and associations, commenced in this world, are renewed, never more to suffer interruption. In the meantime, let us have patience, and wait courageously until the bell for our departure tolls; we shall then go to the place where our friends have already arrived, and since we have cordially loved them, let us continue to love them; let us do, for love of them, that which they wished we should do, and for ourselves, that which they now desire.

However, I am on my guard against saying, "Do not weep," for it is very just that you should weep a little, as a testimony to the sincere affection you bear towards the dear departed. This will be to imitate Jesus Christ, who wept a little over Lazarus, His good friend; but it is on condition that those exterior demonstrations should be moderate, and that those sighs and sobs should not be so much tokens of regret as marks of tenderness.

Let us not weep like those who, altogether attached to this life, consider not that we go to eternity, where, if we shall have lived well in this life, we shall meet again our dear departed, never more to be separated from them. We are not able to prevent our poor heart from feeling the loss of those, who were here below our amiable companions; but still, we must not break the solemn resolution we have taken, to keep our will inseparably united to that of God, nor cease to say to Divine Providence, "Yes, Thou art blessed, for all that which pleases Thee is good." I weep on such occasions, and my heart, which is like a stone on heavenly things, pours out tears over such subjects. The imaginary insensibility of those who do not wish us to be men has always appeared to me chimerical; but, at the same time, after we have paid our tribute to the inferior part of the soul, we must do our duty to the superior part, in which is seated, as on a throne, the spirit of faith, which ought to console us in our afflictions, and even by our afflictions. Blessed are they who rejoice in being afflicted, and who thus transform quassia into honey! God be praised! It is always with tranquility I weep, always with a great sentiment of loving confidence in Divine Providence; for since Our Lord loved death and delivered it as an object for our love, I cannot wish it ill, for taking away my sisters and others, provided that they die in the love of the holy death of the Saviour. I regard this frail life as such a trifle, that I never turn to God with sweeter sentiments of love, than when He has stricken me or permitted me to be afflicted.

I presume you have so much love and fear of God, that seeing His good pleasure and His holy will, you accommodate yourself to them, and sweeten your grief by the consideration of the miseries of this world. We cannot prevent ourselves from feeling much regret at separation; and this regret is not forbidden us, provided we moderate it with the hope of not remaining entirely separated, but consider that in a little time we shall follow our friends to Heaven, the place of our repose, God showing us this mercy.

Raise up your eyes often to Heaven; and see that this life is only a passage to eternity. Four or five months' absence will soon be over. And if our senses, amused with beholding and prizing this world and its life, make us resent a little too sharply that which is contrary to us, let us often correct this defect by the light of faith, which ought to make us judge those most happy who in the fewest days have finished their voyage. Oh, how desirable is eternity, at the cost of some miserable vicissitudes! . . . Every day my soul grows in love and esteem for eternal things. . . . Let time flow by, with which we hasten on to be transformed into the glory of the children of God. . . . How incomparably more amiable is eternity, since its duration is without end, and its days are without nights, and its contentments are without variation!

Oh, if once we had our heart well penetrated with the thought of this holy and blessed eternity: "Go," we should say to our friends, "Go, dear friends, to the Supreme Being, at the hour which the King of Eternity has marked; we shall follow after you, and since time is given us only for this purpose, and the world is peopled only to people Heaven, we will do all that we can to render ourselves worthy of it."

Yes, truly, the journey of our friends to a better life is

most amiable, since it happens only to people Heaven, and to increase the glory of our King; one day we shall go to rejoin them; and, while awaiting that day, let us carefully learn the canticle of holy love, that we may be able to sing it more perfectly in eternity. Blessed are they who place not their confidence in the present life—who esteem it only as a plank by which to pass to the celestial life, in which alone we should center all our hopes!

Let David weep over his Absalom, hanged and lost; but, over the departure of him who has accepted death willingly, who has received the efficacious remedies of the holy Church before dying, there is more occasion to be consoled than afflicted; for, having lived well, he is not dead, but saved from death, since virtuous men do not die, living in Heaven by the magnificent recompense of their merits, and on earth by the glorious memory of their good deeds.

Oh, if we could hear the sweet and amiable words of some deceased one now happy, he would say to us: "My dearly beloved, I beseech you to consider that I am in the place which I so much desired, where I am consoled for all my past labors, which have merited for me the glory of immortality. Why do you not console yourselves with me? When I was on earth, you made profession of loving me, and sometimes seeing me succeed happily, you rejoiced and congratulated with me. Ah! Am I not always the same person? Why then are you afflicted at my departure, since God has given me so much glory? No, I desire everything else from you but sorrow and regret. If you have tears, keep them to weep over the miseries of the world, and also over your sins. Do you not know that the evils of the wretched life in which you live are such, that you ought rather to praise God for having taken me away from them than be dejected? The first who leave it, only find themselves the more fortunate, when they have lived with care of their salvation. No one is esteemed before God for having lived long, but for having lived well. A single anxiety now presses on me: it is, that you should despise, being in the body, those things of which you shall have no more need when out of the body, and that you so live amid the prosperity of the world, that you may not dread its adversity, assuring yourselves that you shall very soon meet again with your dear departed ones, never more to be separated from them through all eternity."

Would to God that all the children of Adam reflected attentively on these beautiful truths! Certainly they would not be so ardent or so eager after pleasures and vanities; for they would see clearly that all they have esteemed until the present is nothing but nothingness, the wages of death, the lure of Satan, the bait of Hell, and by means of this clear knowledge, united with a firm and determined resolution, they would draw from temporal death, help and succor to avoid the eternal.

It is related that Alexander the Great, sailing on the high seas, first and of himself, discovered Arabia Felix, by the odor of the aromatical woods which grew there; and thus formed the desire of conquering the country. In like manner, those who seek the eternal country, though sailing on the high seas of worldly business, have a certain foretaste of Heaven, which wonderfully animates and encourages them, but it is necessary to stand at the bows, and to turn towards that side.

Chapter Two

To a Poor Mother, on the Death of Her Child in Infancy

BEHOLD, my dear daughter, your son is secure; he possesses the everlasting crown. Behold him escaped, and preserved from the risk of being lost, to which we see so many persons exposed. Tell me, might he not with age have become a debauchee? Might you not have received much grief from him, if he had lived, as so many other mothers have received from their children? For, my daughter, we often receive it from those from whom we least expect it. And now God has drawn him away from all these dangers, making him gather the fruits of victory without battle, and reap the harvest of glory without labor.

In your own opinion, my dear daughter, are not your vows and your devotions well recompensed? You made them for him, but that he might remain with you in this valley of tears. Our Lord, who understands best what is good for us, has heard your prayers in favor of the child for whom you offered them, but at the expense of the temporal contentments which you sought.

In truth, I approve very much of the confession you make, that it is on account of your sins this child has been taken away, for this proceeds from humility; but still, I do not believe that it is grounded on truth. No, my dear daughter, it is not to chastise you, but to favor this child, that God has saved it so soon. At the close of our days, when our eyes are opened, we shall see that this life is so little a thing, that we need not regret those who lose it first; the shortest is about the best, provided it conducts to the eternal.

But come, behold your little child in Heaven, among the angels and the Holy Innocents. It knows the pleasure you took in caring for it, during the brief time you had it in charge, and, above all, the devotions you practiced for it; in return, it prays to God for you, and sends up a thousand good wishes for your life, that it may be made more and more conformable to the celestial will, and that you may thus gain the happiness which it enjoys. Remain in peace, my dearest daughter, and keep your heart in Heaven, where you possess this brave little saint. Persevere in desiring always to love more and more faithfully the supreme will.[1]

Oh, how happy for this child to have flown away to

---

1   "I beseech you to unite your sorrow with that of the Blessed Virgin and St. Joseph, when they lost their dearest Child; and remember that Our Lord, on His side, sacrificed the most reasonable feelings of the holiest and most affectionate youth in the world, because He looked to the interests of His Father, which He preferred to the sentiments and tendernesses of human nature."—*Olier.*

Heaven like a little angel, almost before having touched the earth! What a pledge you have on high, my dearest daughter! But I am sure you have treated heart to heart with our Saviour on this affair, and that He has already soothed the natural tenderness of your mother's love, and that you have many times pronounced, with all your heart, the filial protestation which Our Lord has taught us: "Yea, Eternal Father, for so it hath pleased Thee, and it is good that it should be so."

O my daughter, if you have done this, you are happily dead with your child in our Divine Saviour, *and your life is hidden with him in God; and when He will appear, who is your life, you also shall appear with Him in glory.* This is the mode of speaking adopted by the Holy Ghost in Scripture.

We suffer, we die with those whom we love, by the affection that binds us to them; and when they suffer and die in Our Lord, and we acquiesce by patience in their sufferings and demise, for love of Him who, for love of us, was pleased to suffer and to die, we suffer and die with them: all these pains amassed, my dearest daughter, are inestimable spiritual riches, as we shall one day know when, for light labors we shall behold eternal recompenses.

Employ the greatness of your courage to moderate the greatness of the grief which the greatness of your loss has occasioned you. Let us sweetly acquiesce in the decrees of Providence, which are always just, always holy, always adorable, though dark and impenetrable to us.

CHAPTER THREE

TO A FATHER, ON THE
DEATH OF HIS SON

YOU have considered well that this dear child belonged
to God more than to you, who held him only in trust
from the sovereign liberality. And if Providence has judged
that it was time to withdraw him, we must believe that it
has acted thus for his good, in which so fond a father as
you takes such delight. Our life is not so pleasant that those
who escape from it need be much lamented. It appears to
me that this son has gained much for himself by leaving the
world almost before he had arrived in it.[1]

The name of death is terrible, as it is usually proposed
to us, for someone says: "Your dear father is dead," or "Your

---

1   "Why do we weep over those who weep no more, whose tears God has forever wiped
     away? It is over ourselves we ought to weep, and from ourselves extend this compas-
     sion to humanity in general. Faith assures us that we shall soon be reunited with
     those whom our senses represent to us as lost. Live by faith, without listening to flesh
     and blood. In our common center, which is the bosom of God, you will again find
     the person who has disappeared from your eyes."—*Fenelon.*

son is dead." This is not well spoken among Christians. We should say, "Your son or your father is gone to his country and to yours; and because necessity required it, he passed by the way of death, in which he lingered not." I certainly do not know how we can regard as our country this world, in which we remain for so short a time, compared with Heaven, in which we shall dwell forever. Let us go forward then, and be more assured of the presence of our dear friends who are above, than of those who are here below; for, these allow us to go, and delay as long as they can after us, and if they go like us, it is against their choice.

And if any remains of sadness still weight down your mind for the departure of this sweet soul, cast yourself on your knees before the Heart of our crucified Saviour, and ask His assistance. He will give it to you, and will inspire you with the thought and the resolution to prepare yourself well to make in your turn, at the appointed hour, the same passage, by which you may happily arrive at the place where we ought to hope our poor but blessed deceased is now safely lodged.

Chapter Four

To a Mother, on the Death of Her Son Killed in War

HOW much is my soul in pain for your heart, my dearest mother! For I seem to see this poor maternal heart, all filled with an excessive anguish; an anguish, yet, which we cannot blame, or consider strange, if we remember how amiable was this son, whose second removal from among us is now the subject of our affliction.

My dearest mother, it is true, this dear son was one of the most amiable that ever lived; all who knew him knew it, and acknowledged it. But is not this a great part of the consolation we ought now to feel, my dearest mother? For, in truth, it seems to me, that those whose lives are worthy of memory and esteem, live even after their departure; since we take so much pleasure in calling them to mind, and representing them to the minds of those who still remain.

He is gone from this world into that which is the most

desirable of all, and to which we must all go, everyone in his season, and where you will see him sooner than you would perhaps have seen him, if he had remained in this new world amid the fatigues of conquest, which he undertook for his king and for the Church.

In a word, he has ended his mortal days in his duty, and in the obligations of his word. This kind of end is excellent, and we should not doubt but that the great God has rendered it happy, as He continually favored him, from the cradle, with His grace to live in a most Christian manner.

We should enter into the designs of the admirable Providence of God, and rest in its ordinances, with a holy confidence, that it does all things for the best, and perhaps has purified this good soul here by the fire of war, to save it from that of Purgatory.

In short, we may allow afflictions to enter our hearts, but we must not allow them to take up their residence there. God, your good angel, and the wisdom you have acquired by long experience, will suggest these thoughts better to you than anything I could say.

Behold yourself now divested and deprived of the most beautiful garment you ever wore. Bless the name of God who gave it, and who has taken it away; and His Divine Majesty will hold the place of children to you.

Be consoled, my dearest mother, and let your mind be solaced, adoring the Divine Providence, which does all things most sweetly; and, though the motives of its decrees are hidden, yet the certainty of its benignity is manifest, and obliges us to believe that it does everything in perfect goodness. I would willingly say to you, as a remedy for your sorrow, that he who would exempt his heart from the ills of earth, must conceal it in Heaven; and, as David says, "We must hide our soul in the secret of God's countenance, and in the depth of His holy tabernacle." Look well to eternity, to which you tend. You will find that whatever does not refer to that unending duration should not affect your courage. This dear son has passed from one world to another, under good auspices, in the fulfillment of his duty towards God and the king; no longer look upon this journey but in the light of eternity.

Let us not be grieved, my daughter, we shall soon be all reunited. We advance continually, and draw near to that country where our departed ones are, and, in two or three moments, we shall arrive there. Place your heart, I beg of you, my dearest daughter, at the foot of the cross, and accept the death and the life of all those whom you love, for love of Him who gave His life and received His death for you.

You are almost ready to start to the place where this amiable child now dwells; but, while awaiting the hour of setting sail, calm your maternal heart, by the consideration of that holy eternity to which he has gone, and to which you are going. Though you cannot write to him sometimes as you would wish, you can speak to God for him, and he will immediately know all that you would wish him to know, and will receive all the assistance which you may render to him, by devotions and good works, as soon as you will have performed and delivered them into the hands of His Divine Majesty.

Repress your too eager desire to know where this dear

deceased one now is, in the other life; and, when you find your mind engaged on this pursuit, you should instantly turn it to Our Lord, with these or the like words: "O Lord, how sweet is Thy Providence, and how good is Thy mercy! Oh, how happy for this dear child to have fallen into Thy paternal arms, where he cannot but be safe, in whatever place he is!"

Yes, for it is necessary to guard against thinking of any other place than Paradise or Purgatory, since, thanks be to God! There is no reason for thinking otherwise. Withdraw then your mind thus, and employ it in acts of love towards our crucified Lord.

When you recommend this child to the Divine Majesty, say simply: "O Lord, I recommend to Thee the child of my bowels, but much more the child of the bowels of Thy mercy, formed of my blood, but redeemed by Thine."

CHAPTER FIVE

TO A LADY, ON THE
DEATH OF HER FATHER

BUT now, my very dear daughter, it is necessary that your heart should henceforward endure the absence of your good father, since Divine Providence has been pleased at length to draw him out of this miserable mortal life, in which we live dying, and continually die living.

As for me, my daughter, I do not wish to present you with any other consolation than that of Jesus Christ crucified, at the sight of whom, your faith will console you; for, after the death of our Saviour, every death is happy to those who, like the deceased of whom I speak, die within the pale and with the assistance of Holy Church; and whoever glories in the death of Our Lord will never be afflicted at the death of those whom He has redeemed and received as His own.[1]

---

1 "While depriving you of creatures, the Lord wishes that His dear Son should hold the

19

I am accustomed to say to all the souls who address themselves to me, that we must lift up our hearts on high, as the Church says, during the Holy Sacrifice. Live then with great and generous thoughts, attached to that holy Providence, which disposes of mortal moments only in order to [bring about] eternal life.

The heart thus nobly lifted up is always humble, for it is established on truth, and not on vanity; it is sweet and peaceful, for it makes no account of that which might trouble it. But when I say that it is sweet and peaceful, I do not mean to say that it has no sorrows or sentiments of affliction. No, indeed, my dear daughter, I do not say that; but, I say that sufferings, pains, tribulations, are all accompanied with such a strong resolution to endure them for God, that their bitterness, however bitter it may be, is received in peace and tranquility.

As for the rest, this grievous separation is so much the less hard, as it will continue for the less time, and we not only expect, but we aspire to that happy repose in which this beautiful soul is now, or will soon be, lodged; let us accept, I beseech you, agreeably the little delay we must make here below, and, instead of multiplying tears over ourselves, offer them for it to Our Lord, that He may be

---

place of all persons and things to you. It is at this hour that He will increase His love in you, and make you feel that He wishes to be your father, as well as your spouse and faithful friend; in a word, that He wishes to be all things to you. Herein appears the holy jealousy of Jesus, incomparable in love."—*Olier.*

pleased to hasten its reception into the arms of His divine goodness, if He has not already granted it this grace.[2]

---

2   "It is God, as the Apostle says, who consoles the afflicted and the humbled, and supports them through all their desolations. What a happiness that everything in Christianity binds us to God, and that nothing happens to the children of this Father, which does not render them His by a new title! The condition of an orphan must make you more dependent on God, more retired into Him, and more separated from all else, and establish you in a greater confidence towards Him, and in a more perfect spirit of abandonment. Let the eternal bosom of God be now your abode, your repose, your comfort, your strength, your counsel, your light, your love, your life, your all, and let it begin to be to you on earth what it will be to you for an eternity in Heaven. Losing the image you will find the reality; and this Divine Father, from whom proceeds all paternity, in Heaven and on earth, will be all things to you, as He is to His Son, and to His well-beloved daughter: I mean Jesus and Mary, from whom I conjure you to be inseparable, and in whose society, to seek refuge, when creatures besiege and attack you."—*Olier.*

Chapter Six

To a Lady, on the Death of Her Husband

MY GOD! How frail is this life, and how fleeting are its consolations! One moment they appear, and the next they are gone, and, if it were not for the holy eternity to which all our days tend, we should have much reason indeed to mourn over our human condition.

The thoughts of men are vain and useless, to comfort a heart so much afflicted as yours. God alone is the master and consoler of hearts. He alone calms souls of good will, that is to say, those who hope in Him.

The interior words spoken by God to the afflicted heart, which has recourse to His goodness, are sweeter than honey, and more salutary than the most precious balm.

The heart that is united to the Heart of God cannot be prevented from loving, and accepting lovingly, the arrows which His hand shoots at it.

For so long a time you have served God, and studied in the school of His cross, that you ought to accept this cross, not only patiently, but sweetly and affectionately, in consideration of Him who bore His, and was borne upon it, even to death; and of her who, having only one Son, but a Son of incomparable love, saw Him die on the cross, with eyes full of tears and a heart full of sorrow, yet a sweet sorrow, in favor of our salvation, and that of the whole world.

Now, the Sovereign Goodness will undoubtedly incline towards you, and come into your heart to aid you in this tribulation, if you cast yourself into its arms, and resign yourself into its paternal hands.

God gave you this husband; He has taken him away, withdrawing him to Himself. He is obliged to be favorable to you in your afflictions.

All things considered, we must accommodate our hearts to the conditions of the present life. It is a perishable life; and death, which rules over it, observes no regular order, sometimes taking here, sometimes there, without any preference or method, the good among the bad, and the young among the old.

Oh, how blessed are they who, living in continual mistrust of death, are always ready to die, that so they may be able to live forever in that life, where there is no more death!

Assuredly, my dear lady, the greatest desire your husband had at his departure was, that you should not languish long in the regret which his absence would cause you, but that you should endeavor to moderate, for love of him, the affection which his love gave you; and now, in the happiness which he enjoys, or which he confidently awaits, he wishes you a holy consolation, and that, assuaging your tribulation, you should preserve your eyes for some better employment than that of tears, and your mind for some more desirable occupation than that of sadness.

And since true friendship makes us rejoice in the just satisfaction of our friend, I beg of you, to please your husband, console yourself, solace your mind, and raise your courage. And, if the counsel I give you with the utmost sincerity is agreeable to you, practice it, prostrating yourself before Our Lord, acquiescing in His appointments, considering the soul of this dear deceased as desiring for yours a true and Christian fortitude, abandoning yourself entirely to the celestial vigilance of the Saviour of your soul, your Protector, who will aid and succor you, and at length restore you to your departed one, not as a wife to her husband, but as an heir of Heaven to a co-heir.

Little by little, God severs us from the contentments of this world; we must, then, more ardently aspire after those of immortality, and keep our hearts lifted up to Heaven, where our expectations are settled, and where we have already a great many of the friends we love. May the name of Our Lord be forever blessed, and may His love ever live and reign in the midst of our hearts!

CHAPTER SEVEN

ON THE DEATH OF A BROTHER

MY DEAR brother (for I am in the place of him whom our good God has taken to be near Himself), I am told that you weep continually for this truly sensible separation. There is no necessity that this should be so; either you weep for him, or for yourself: if for him, why weep, since our brother is in Paradise, where tears are unknown? If for yourself, is there not self-love in it?

I speak freely with you, inasmuch as one would suppose you loved your own more than his happiness, which is beyond conception. And would you wish that, on your account, he should not be with Him, *who gives us life, motion, and being—us,* especially, who acquiesce in His holy pleasure and divine will?

But come to see us, and frequently, and we shall change tears into joy, remembering together that in which our good brother rejoices, and which will never be taken away from him; and, in fine, think often thus thereon and on him, and you will live joyful, as I desire for you with all my heart.

Chapter Eight

On the Death of a Father

O MY dearest daughter, what can I say to you on this departure? I doubt not but God has care of your heart, in these occurrences, and that if He wounds with one hand, He applies His balm with the other: *He strikes and heals, He kills and makes alive;* and so long as we can lift up our eyes, and behold the celestial Providence, anguish cannot overwhelm us. But enough, my dearest daughter; God and your good angel having consoled you, I shall not put my hand to it: *your most bitter bitterness is in peace.* What need is there for still speaking of it? In proportion as God draws to Himself, piece after piece, the treasures which our heart had collected here below, that is to say, those whom we loved, He draws our heart itself thither too. "And since I have no longer a father," said St. Francis, "I shall say more freely: Our Father, Who art in Heaven." My dearest daughter, often extend your views even to Heaven.

We are wrong, if we regard our parents, our friends, our contentments, as objects on which we can establish our hearts. Are we, I ask you, in this world on any other conditions than those of the rest of men, or than those of the perpetual inconstancy in which everything has been established? We must repose our intentions on the holy eternity to which we aspire. O peace of the human heart! Nowhere to be found but in glory and on the cross of Jesus Christ! Live thus; and often rejoice your heart with the confident expectation of enjoying forever a blessed and immutable immortality.

CHAPTER NINE

———————————

HOW MUCH THE THOUGHT OF HEAVEN OUGHT TO CONSOLE US

THE end of man is the clear vision and enjoyment of God, which he hopes to obtain in Heaven. Blessed then is he who employs this short mortal life to acquire an eternal good, referring the transitory days here below to the day of immortality, and applying all the perishable moments which remain to him, to gain a holy eternity. The true light of Heaven will not fail to show him the secure course, and to conduct him happily into the harbor of everlasting felicity.[1]

———————————

1 "My son, lift up your eyes to Heaven to see your reward," cried out the heroic mother of young Symphorian, expiring in the midst of the most cruel torments. There is no pain that the sight of Heaven does not sweeten, no sorrow that it does not soothe, no tears that it does not wipe away, no murmurs that it does not appease. There is nothing so bitter but it becomes sweet in the hope of eternal goods.

The Apostle St. Paul himself often thought on this glorious recompense, to find encouragement in the midst of the tribulations which pressed upon him from every side. "The time of my deliverance draws nigh," he said to one of his disciples; "I have finished my course, I have kept the faith, it only remains for me to await the

The rivers flow incessantly, and as the Wise Man says, return to the sea, which is the place of their nativity, and is also their last resting place; all their motion tends only to unite them with their original source. "O God," says St. Augustine, "Thou hast created my heart for Thyself, and never can it find repose but in Thee." *What have I in heaven, and what do I desire on earth, but Thee, my God? Thou art the God of my heart, and my portion forever.* Behold in detail a few points which we have to believe on this subject:

Firstly, there is a Paradise, a place of eternal glory, a most perfect state, in which all goods are assembled, and where there is no evil; a world of wonders, replete with felicity, incomparable in happiness, infinitely surpassing every expectation; the house of God and the palace of the blessed; a most lovely and desirable city; and so precious that all the beauties of the world put together are nothing in comparison with its excellence: so that no one can conceive the infinite greatness of the abysses of its delights.

Consider that, for an eternity, the fortunate souls there will enjoy the happiness of seeing God give Himself all to all, and hearing the eternal Son say benignly to His Father: "My Father, I wish that those whom Thou hast given Me may be eternally with Me, and that they may see the glory which I have had from Thee before the creation of the world;" and turning to His dear children: "Did I not tell you that whoever would love Me, would be loved by My Father, and that we would manifest ourselves to him?" Then this holy company, inundated with pleasure in the bosom of the

---

crown which is reserved for me, which the Lord, as a just judge, will render me on the great day."

Divinity, will sing the eternal *alleluia* of joy and praise to its Creator.

Secondly, the soul, purified from all sin, entering Heaven, will that instant behold God Himself, unveiled, face to face, as He is: contemplating, by a view of true and real presence, the proper divine essence, and in it infinite beauties.

The sweet St. Bernard, while yet young, being at Chatillon-sur-Seine, on Christmas night, waited in the church until the commencement of the Divine Office; as the poor child waited, he fell into a light slumber, during which (O my God, what a happiness!) he saw in spirit, and the vision was quite clear and distinct, how the Son of God, having espoused human nature, and become a little infant in the bowels of His Mother, was, with an humble gentleness and a celestial majesty, virginally born of her sacred womb: a vision which so filled his heart with jubilation, that all his life he had a tender recollection of it, and the thought of the mystery of the nativity of his Master, always brought him spiritual joy and extraordinary consolation.

Alas! If an unsubstantial vision of the temporal birth of the Son of God so powerfully ravished and delighted the heart of a child, what will it be when our minds, gloriously illumined by the blessed light of glory, will see that eternal birth, by which the Son proceeds, true God of true God, divinely and eternally born of the Father? Then will the soul be deified, filled with God, and made like to God, by an eternal and immutable participation of God, uniting Himself to it as fire does to the iron which it penetrates, communicating its light, brilliancy, heat, and other qualities, in such a manner that both seem one and the same fire.

As God has given us the light of reason, by which we can know Him as the author of nature, and the light of faith, by which we consider Him as the source of grace, so He will give us the light of glory, by which we shall contemplate Him as the fountain of beatitude and life eternal, yet a fountain that we shall not contemplate from afar, as we now do by the light of faith, but a fountain that we shall see by the light of glory, plunged and lost in it.

Thirdly, the soul will be happy forever amid the nobility and variety of the citizens and inhabitants of that blessed country, with its millions of millions of angels, of cherubim, of seraphim, its troop of apostles, of martyrs, of confessors, of virgins, of holy women, whose number is without number! Oh, how happy is this company! The least of the blessed is more beautiful to behold than the whole world. What will it be to see them all? They sing the sweet canticle of eternal love, they ever rejoice in an unceasing gladness, they interchange unspeakable contentments, and they live in the consolations of a happy and indissoluble society.

But, O God! If sincere human friendship is so agreeable, what will it be to behold the reciprocal love of the blessed? Certainly, the hearts of the citizens of Heaven will be abyssed in love, through admiration of the beauty and sweetness of such a love!

Fourthly, in Paradise God will give Himself all to all, and not in parts, since He is a whole which has no parts; but still, He will give Himself variously, and with as many differences, as there will be blessed guests. As star differs from star in brightness, so men will be different, one from the other, in glory, in proportion as they will have been different in graces and merits; and as there are probably no two men equal in charity in this world, so there will probably be no two equal in glory in the next.

Consider how delightful it must be to see that city where the great King sits on the throne of His Majesty, surrounded by all His blessed servants; there are found the choirs of angels, and the company of celestial men; there are found the venerable troop of the prophets, the chosen number of the apostles, the victorious army of innumerable martyrs, the august rank of pontiffs, the sacred flock of confessors, the true and perfect religious, the holy women, the humble widows, the pure virgins. The glory of every one is not equal, but nevertheless they all taste one and the same pleasure, for there is the reign of full and perfect charity.

One ray of glory, one drop of the love of the blessed, is of more value, has more efficacy, and merits more esteem, than all other kinds of knowledge and love which ever could enter into the hearts of mortal men.

Fifthly, notwithstanding the variety and diversity of glory, yet each blessed soul, contemplating the infinite beauty of God, and the abyss of infinity that remains to be seen in this same beauty, feels perfectly satisfied and satiated, and is content with the glory it enjoys, according to the rank it holds in Heaven, on account of the most amiable Divine Providence, which has so arranged everything.

What a joy to be environed on all sides with incredible pleasures, and, as a most happy bird, to fly and sing forever in the air of the Divinity! What a favor, after a million of languors, pains, and fatigues, endured in this mortal life, after endless desires for the eternal truth, never fully satisfied in this world, to see oneself in the haven of all tranquility, and to have at length reached the living and mighty source of the fresh waters of undying life, which alone can extinguish the passions, and satiate the human heart.[2]

We ought always to have the eternal days in our mind; and, in consideration of them, nothing will appear impossible. Did not David say, "Because of the words of Thy mouth, I have walked in hard and difficult ways"? And what are the words of the lips of Our Lord, if not the words of eternal life? St. Peter had reason to say: "To whom, O Lord, shall we go? Thou hast the words of eternal life."

This is that eternal life, to which Our Lord in Genesis wished to move Cain, when He said to him: "If thou do well, shalt thou not receive recompense?" This is that eternal life, for which the good man Jacob called himself a pilgrim. "The days," he answered King Pharaoh, "of my pilgrimage are a hundred and thirty years, few and evil, and they are not come up to the days of the pilgrimage of my fathers." "I am mindful of the ancient days, and I have in my thoughts the eternal years." Eternal life, when well considered, is sufficient to move the hardest hearts.

In the beginning, during the first fervor of the Order

---

2 "The predestined are more happy in Heaven than the reprobate are miserable in Hell, God being more generous in rewarding, than severe in punishing. In its effects, mercy every way surpasses justice. Yes, the joy of the blessed in Heaven is immense, and this is precisely what rendered the realization of the rich man's desire impossible, when he asked for one drop of water from Heaven to be laid on his tongue by Lazarus. A single drop of the celestial joy falling into the abode of the reprobate, would suffice to extinguish its flames, and to convert into sweetness all its bitterness."—*Ventura*.

of St. Dominic, there was a preacher named Reginald, who preached at Bologne with incredible fruit. There was in the city a learned and rich man, who, for fear of being converted, would not attend a single sermon, though others flocked in crowds. At length, however, he ventured on St. Stephen's Day, and, hearing a discourse on the words: "I see the heavens opened," he was converted, and became a religious.

For eternal life, David inclined his will and his heart to observe the commandments of God; St. Augustine wished to retire among his religious, before being made bishop; St. John the Baptist dwelt in the desert.

CHAPTER TEN

HOW AGREEABLE IT WILL BE TO
PARENTS AND FRIENDS TO
MEET AGAIN AND CONVERSE
TOGETHER IN HEAVEN

ALL the blessed know one another in Heaven, and by
their names, as the Gospel gives us to understand,
since, in the little specimen of it which Our Lord was
pleased to show on Thabor to His Apostles, He wishes that
they should know Moses and Elias, whom they had never
seen before.

But if it is thus, what contentment shall we receive in
meeting again with those whom we have so dearly loved
in this life, where we shall even know the new Christians
who are now being converted to the Faith in the Indies, in
Japan, at the Antipodes! And holy friendships, commenced
for God in this life, will be continued in the next forever.

We shall love particular persons, but these particular

friendships will not give rise to particularities; for all our friendships will take their origin in the charity of God, who, guiding them all, will dispose that we shall love every blessed soul with that pure love with which we ourselves shall be loved by the divine goodness.

O God, what consolation shall we derive from the celestial conversation that we shall hold one with another! There, our good angels will afford us a consolation greater than can be told or conceived, when they will introduce themselves to us, and represent to us so lovingly the care they had of our salvation during the course of our mortal life, reminding us of the holy inspirations which they brought us, as a sacred milk which they had drawn from the bosom of the divine beauty, to gain us to the pursuit of those divine sweetnesses in which we shall then rejoice. "Do you not remember," they will say to us, "such an inspiration that I brought you at such a time, reading such a book, listening to such a sermon, looking on such an image, as happened to St. Mary of Egypt, an inspiration that incited you to be converted to Our Lord, and was the ground of your predestination?" O God, will not our hearts be then plunged in unutterable happiness?

But, besides, every one of the blessed will have a particular intercourse with the others, according to his rank and dignity. St. Augustine expressed a wish one day that he could see Rome exulting in a glorious triumph, St. Paul preaching, or Our Lord conversing among the people, healing the sick, and performing various miracles. O God, what consolation for this great saint, to see the celestial Jerusalem rejoicing in its divine triumph, and the great Apostle

St. Paul intoning with wondrous melody those praises which he will forever sing to the Divine Majesty in Heaven! But what an excess of consolation for St. Augustine, to see the perpetual miracle of the felicity of the blessed, performed by Our Lord, having raised us from the dead! Imagine the pleasant conversation which these two saints will have with each other, St. Paul saying to St. Augustine: "My dear brother, do you not remember that, while reading my epistle, you were touched with such an inspiration, which solicited you to be converted, an inspiration which I had obtained from the mercy of our good God, by the prayers I made for you at the same time when you were reading what I had written?" Will not the heart of this holy father be then inundated with ineffable sweetness?

O God, what a consolation shall we receive, being in Heaven, when we shall see the blessed face of Our Lady, all inflamed with the love of God. And if St. Elizabeth was transported with joy and delight, when, one day being visited by her, she heard Our Lady intone the sacred canticle: *Magnificat anima mea Dominum,* how much more will our minds and hearts thrill with unspeakable rapture when we shall hear intoned, by this divine *cantatrice,* the beautiful songs of everlasting love!

O God, what sweet melody! Undoubtedly we shall faint in inconceivable joys.

But, you will say to me, since we shall converse with all those who will be in the heavenly Jerusalem, what shall we say? Of what shall we speak? What will be the subject of our intercourse? O God, what the subject! It will be of the mercy of God to us here below, by which He rendered us capable of entering into the enjoyment of a blessed felicity, in which the soul will have nothing more to desire; for, under the name of felicity are comprised all kinds of goods, which, yet, are one only good, consisting in the enjoyment of God.

But again, of what shall we treat in our conversation? Of the death and Passion of Our Lord. Do we not learn it in the Transfiguration, where He speaks of nothing so much as of the success He should accomplish in Jerusalem, an excess no other than the death of this divine Saviour? Oh, if we could comprehend what a consolation the blessed feel in speaking of this death, how much our souls would delight in thinking of it!

Let us pass still further, I pray you, and say something of the honor we shall have in speaking to Our Lord Himself. Oh, here indeed our felicity will take an amazing increase. What shall we do, dear souls, what will become of us, I ask you, when we shall see the most adorable and amiable Heart of our Divine Master, through the sacred wound of His side, all burning with the love He bears us, a Heart in which we shall see our names written in letters of love? Oh, is it possible, we shall then say to our divine Saviour, that Thou hast loved us so much as to engrave our very names on Thy Heart and Thy hands? Still it is most true. The prophet Isaias, speaking in the person of Our Lord, says: "Though a mother should forget the child which she has borne in her womb, yet I will never forget thee, for I have engraven thy name on My hands." But Our Lord, improving on these words, will say to us: "Not only have I engraven thy name on My hands, but also on My

Heart." A subject, indeed, of the greatest consolation, to see that we are so dearly beloved by Our Lord, and that He always carries us on His Heart! Oh, what wonderful delight for every one of the blessed spirits, when they will see in this most sacred and adorable Heart, the thoughts of peace which He had for them, even at the hour of His Passion, thoughts by which He prepared for us not only the principal means of our salvation, but also in particular, with admirable goodness, all the divine attractions and holy inspirations by which this sweetest Saviour would draw us to His love! Will not this sight, this consideration, which we shall make on the sacred love of our sovereign Master, by whom we have been so fondly and so ardently loved, inflame our hearts with unparalleled love and affection? What ought we not to do, in order to enjoy such exquisite and ineffable happiness?

If during this mortal life, when we hear that which we have spoken of, we find so much contentment that we can scarcely cease from thinking of it, what joy and what jubilation shall we feel, when we hear resounding, through the courts of Heaven, the loud praises of the Divine Majesty, whom we ought to love and shall then love more than it is possible for us to express or comprehend? And if, during this life, we take so much pleasure in the mere thought of eternal felicity, how much more pleasure shall we feel in the enjoyment of this same felicity, a felicity which will never have an end, a glory which will continue forever, without the possibility of our being ejected from it? Oh, how much this security will increase our bliss and our consolation!

Let us then walk gaily and joyously amid the difficulties

of this transitory life; let us, with open arms, embrace mortifications, pains, and afflictions, if we meet them on our way, since we are assured that these pains will have an end, and that they will terminate with our life, after which there will be nothing more left but joy and everlasting contentments and consolations.

Believe me, to live content during this pilgrimage, we must keep before our eyes the hope of arriving safely in our country, where we shall abide forever, and in the meantime steadfastly hope; for it is true that God, who calls us to Himself, regards us as we advance, and will never permit anything to happen to us, unless it be for our greater good; He knows what we are, and will keep His paternal hand over us, that nothing may arrest our course.

My God, what consolation I feel in the expectation of beholding us all united in the will of loving and praising God! Let Divine Providence conduct us wherever it pleases; I have a firm hope and assurance that we shall reach the end safely. God be praised! I have this confidence. Let us be joyous in the service of the Divine Majesty; let us be joyous without thoughtlessness, and confident without ignorance.

CHAPTER ELEVEN

WE SHOULD HOPE TO
GO TO HEAVEN[1]

AND if these goods are true, why, O worldlings, do you turn aside from this glorious residence? Why do you abandon the sovereign happiness? Ah, would it not be better to aspire after a day of delicious peace, to retrace your steps towards the path of virtue, to seek an eternal repose, to travel towards the Holy Land that has been promised you, than to wallow in the mire of sin, and to live in the dark atmosphere of the society of the wicked?

---

1 Have confidence through all your trials; forget not that the leaves must fall before the tree becomes green again, that the grain of seed must die in the bosom of the earth before flourishing again above its surface. Yet a few days of patient sorrow, and our transformed mortality will be clothed with immortality, and this corruption will be changed into incorruptible light; and, united with the saints in the place of refreshment and peace, where grief and lamentation are unknown, you will say with them: No, the sufferings of that short time were not worthy to be compared with the glory which has been revealed in us; that fleeting moment, that little portion of tribulation which fell to us, does not equal the eternal weight, the immense measure of happiness which is its fruit and recompense.

45

The whole world invites you to Paradise: your good angel presses you with all his strength, offering you on God's part a thousand helps, a thousand graces; Jesus Christ, from the summit of Heaven, looks down lovingly upon you, and sweetly invites you to the throne of glory, which He has prepared for you in the abundance of His mercy; the Blessed Virgin urges you maternally; the saints, millions of holy souls, exhort you affectionately, and assure you that the way of virtue is not so difficult as the world says it is; will you not accept the favors of Heaven? Will you not correspond with the attractions and inspirations that are presented to you?

Oh, how often we ought, at least on great feasts, to keep our minds fixed on the heavenly Jerusalem, the glorious city of God, where we shall hear His praises ringing from the sweet voices of an endless multitude of saints; and, inquiring of them how they arrived there, we shall learn that the Apostles went chiefly by love, the martyrs by constancy, the doctors by meditation, the confessors by mortification, the virgins by purity of body and soul, and all in general by humility.

God would not have given us souls capable of contemplating and desiring this holy eternity, if He had not intended to bestow on us the means of obtaining it. Hence, then, let our hearts be filled with a sweet confidence, and let us say: We shall do sufficient; no, not we, but the grace of God with us. The more powerful and pressing this desire will be in us, the more enjoyment and contentment will its fulfillment one day bring us.

God be praised! I have this firm confidence in the

depth of my heart, that we shall live forever with God; we shall one day be all together in Heaven; we must take courage; we shall soon be there. And what would Our Lord do with His eternal life, if He would not bestow it on poor and contemptible creatures like us, who have no hope but in His sovereign goodness? O my God, what a consolation I find in the assurance that my heart will be eternally abyssed in the love of the Heart of Jesus! Let Providence conduct us whithersoever it pleases: what matter? We shall arrive safely in the harbor.

Of St. Francis de Sales to the Pious Reader

IT IS with all my heart, I say the word, "Adieu." To God (*A Dieu*) may you ever belong in this life, serving Him faithfully in the midst of the pains we all have in carrying our crosses, and in the immortal life, blessing Him eternally with all the celestial court. The greater good of our souls is to be with God; and the greatest good, to be with God alone.

He who is with God alone, is never sad, unless for having offended God, and his sadness then consists in a profound but tranquil and peaceful humility and submission, after which he rises again in the Divine Goodness, by a sweet and perfect confidence, without chagrin or vexation.

He who is with God alone seeks only God, and because God is no less in tribulation than in prosperity, he remains in peace during times of adversity.

He who is with God alone thinks often of Him in the midst of the occupations of this life.

He who is with God alone would be glad that everyone should know he wishes to serve God, and to be engaged in exercises suitable to keep him united to God.

Live then entirely to God; desire only to please Him, and to please creatures only in Him, and for Him. What greater blessing can I wish you? Thus, then, by this continual wish I make for your soul, I say: Adieu.

To God let us belong, without end, without reserve, without measure, as He is ours forever. May we always unite our little crosses with His great one!

To God let us live, and to God without anything more, since out of Him, and without Him, we seek for nothing: no, not even for ourselves, who, indeed, out of Him, and without Him, are only true nothings.

Adieu. I desire for you the abundance of Divine Love, which is and will be forever the only good of our hearts, given to us only for Him, who has given His Heart entirely to us.

Let Jesus be our crown! Let Mary be our hope! I am, in the name of the Son and the Mother,

Sincerely yours,

FRANCIS DE SALES

SUPPLEMENT

---

1. We Should Not Despair of the Salvation of Any Sinner[1]

S T. FRANCIS de Sales, says the Bishop of Belley, never wished that the repentance of any sinner should be despaired of before his last breath, observing that this life was the way of our pilgrimage, in which those who walked might fall, and those who fell might, by grace, rise again, and, like the giants in the fable, they sometimes rose stronger than they had fallen, grace superabounding where sin had abounded.

He went still further; for, even after death, he did not wish that anyone should pass a bad judgment on those who had led a bad life, unless it regarded those of whose damnation we are assured by the truth of the Holy Scripture. Beyond this point, He would not allow anyone to seek to penetrate into the secrets of God, which are reserved to His wisdom.

---

1 We take this chapter from the *Spirit of St. Francis de Sales,* by Camus [Bishop of Belley].

His principal reason was, that, as the first grace of justification does not fall under the merit of any preceding work, so the last grace, which is that of final perseverance, is not given to any merit either. Besides, who has known the mind of the Lord, and who has been His counselor? For this reason, He wished that, even after the last breath, we should hope well of the deceased person, however sad an end he might have seemed to make, because we can only form very uncertain conjectures, founded on external appearances, in which the most experienced are often deceived.[2]

2. SENTIMENTS OF ST. FRANCIS DE SALES ON THE NUMBER OF THE ELECT

The extreme gentleness of St. Francis de Sales, says the Bishop of Belley, from whom we borrow this chapter, always led him to the mildest opinions, however little probability they carried. We were conversing one day, in company, on this dreadful word of the Gospel: "Many are called, but few are chosen." Someone remarked that the number of the elect was called a little flock, as that of fools, or of the reprobate, was called infinite, and such things. He answered that he thought very few Christians (he spoke of those in the true Church, out of which there is no salvation) would be damned; because, he said, having the root of the True Faith, sooner or later it usually yields its fruit,

---

2 We read the following passage in the *Life of Père De Ravignan:* "In certain deaths there are hidden mysteries of mercy and strokes of grace, in which the eye of man beholds only the strokes of justice. By the gleams of the last light, God reveals Himself to souls whose greatest misfortune was to have been ignorant of Him; and the last sigh, understood by Him who searches hearts, may be a groan that asks for pardon."

which is salvation, and from being dead, becomes living by charity.

And when asked what, then, was the meaning of this word of the Gospel concerning the small number of the elect, he said that in comparison with the rest of the world and with infidel nations, the number of Christians was very small, but that of this small number there would be very few lost, according to this remarkable sentence: *There is no damnation for those who are in Jesus Christ.* (*Rom.* 8:1). Which, indeed, is to be understood of justifying grace;[3] but this grace is not separated from a faith living and animated by charity. Moreover, as He who gives the grace to begin, gives also the grace to perfect the undertaking, so it is credible that the vocation to Christianity, which is a work of God, is a perfect work, and conducts to the end of all consummation, which is glory.

I added another reason, and he was pleased with it: that the mercy of God being above all His works, and swimming over His justice, as oil over vinegar, there was every reason for trusting in His own natural disposition to pity and forgive, abundantly shown forth in the copious redemption of the Saviour; and there was no sign for believing that God would have commenced to erect the salvation of the true Christian by faith, which is its foundation, without proceeding with it to the end, which consists in charity.

This doctrine is of great consolation, provided it does not make us negligent in doing good; for, it is not enough to say with the ancients: *The temple of the Lord, the temple*

---

3 Justifying grace—that is, Sanctifying Grace.—*Publisher,* 2013.

of the Lord—the Church, the Church, I am in the bosom of the true Church. Since the Church is holy, and the pillar of truth, it is our duty to live holily, as well as to believe truly; for, to commit crimes in the house of God, is to defile His sanctuary, and to render oneself doubly guilty. And who is unaware that the servant who knew the will of his Master, and did not trouble himself to perform it, deserved a double chastisement?

We should fear, said St. Francis de Sales, the judgments of God, but without discouragement, and take courage at the sight of His mercies, but without presumption. Those who have an excessive and inordinate fear of being damned show plainly that they have great need of humility and submission. We must indeed abase, annihilate, lose ourselves, but this ought to be to gain, preserve, save ourselves. That humility which is prejudicial to charity, is assuredly a false humility. Such is that which leads to trouble, to discouragement, to despair; for it is contrary to charity, which, while commanding us *to work out our salvation with fear and trembling*, forbids us at the same time to diffide in the goodness of God, who desires the conversion and salvation of all.

3. THE SOULS IN PURGATORY

The opinion of St. Francis de Sales, says the Bishop of Belley, was that, from the thought of Purgatory, we should draw more consolation than pain. The greater number of those, he said, who fear Purgatory so much, do so in consideration of their own interests, and of the love they bear themselves rather than the interests of God, and this happens because those who treat of this place from the pulpit usually speak of its pains, and are silent of the happiness and peace which are found in it.

No doubt the torments are so great that the greatest sufferings of this life cannot be compared with them; but still, the interior satisfaction there is such, that no enjoyment or prosperity on earth can equal it.

The souls in Purgatory are in a constant state of union with God.

They are perfectly submissive to His will, or, to speak better, their will is so transformed into the will of God, that they cannot wish for anything but what God wishes; in such a manner, that if Paradise were opened to them, they would rather precipitate themselves into Hell than appear before God with the stains which they still perceive on themselves.

They are purified voluntarily and lovingly, because such is the divine good pleasure. The souls in Purgatory are there indeed for their sins, sins which they have detested, and sovereignly detested; but as to the abjection and pain that still remain, of being detained there, and deprived for a time of the joy of the blessed in Paradise, they endure all that lovingly, and devoutly pronounce this canticle of the divine justice: "Thou art just, O Lord, and thy judgment is right."

They wish to be there in the manner that pleases God, and for as long a time as He pleases.

They are impeccable, and cannot have the least motion of impatience, or be guilty of the smallest imperfection.

They love God more than themselves, and more than

all things else, with a perfect, pure, and disinterested love.

They are consoled by angels.

They are assured of their salvation.

Their most bitter bitterness is in the most profound peace.

If Purgatory is a kind of Hell as regards pain, it is a kind of Paradise as regards the sweetness which charity diffuses through the heart—charity which is stronger than death, and more powerful than Hell, and whose lamps are fire and flames.

A state more desirable than terrible, since its flames are flames of love.

Terrible, nevertheless, since they postpone the end of all consummation, which consists in seeing and loving God, and in this vision and love, to praise and glorify Him for all eternity. With regard to this subject, St. Francis de Sales approved very much of the admirable *Treatise on Purgatory*, written by the blessed Catherine of Genoa.

If these things be so, I shall be asked, why recommend so much the souls in Purgatory to our charity?

The reason is, because, notwithstanding their advantages, the state of these souls is still very sad and truly deserving of compassion, and, moreover, the glory which they will render to God in Heaven is delayed. These two motives ought to engage us, by our prayers, our fasts, our alms, and all kinds of good works, especially by offering the Holy Sacrifice of the Mass for them, to procure their speedy deliverance.

When any of St. Francis de Sales' friends or acquaintances died, he never grew weary of speaking fondly of them, or recommending them to the prayers of others.

His usual expression was: "We do not remember sufficiently our dead, our faithful departed;" and the proof of it is, that we do not speak enough of them. We turn away from that discourse as from a sad subject, we leave the dead to bury their dead; their memory perishes from us with the sound of their mourning bell; we forget that the friendship which ends, even with death, is never true, Holy Scripture assuring us that true love is stronger than death.

He was accustomed to say that in this single work of mercy, the thirteen others are assembled.

Is it not, he said, in some manner, to visit the sick, to obtain by our prayers the relief of the poor suffering souls in Purgatory?

Is it not to give drink to those who thirst after the vision of God, and who are enveloped in burning flames, to share with them the dew of our prayers?

Is it not to feed the hungry, to aid in their deliverance by the means which faith suggests?

Is it not truly to ransom prisoners?

Is it not to clothe the naked, to procure for them a garment of light, a raiment of glory?

Is it not an admirable degree of hospitality, to procure their admission into the heavenly Jerusalem, and to make them fellow citizens with the saints and domestics of God?

Is it not a greater service to place souls in Heaven, than to bury bodies in the earth?

As to spirituals, is it not a work whose merit may be compared to that of counseling the weak, correcting the wayward, instructing the ignorant, forgiving offences, enduring injuries? And what consolation, however great, that can be given to the afflicted of this world, is comparable with that which is brought by our prayers, to those poor souls who have such bitter need of them?

4. Motives on account of which Imperfect Christians Ought Not to Fear Their Passage to Eternity, and May Even Desire It [4]

As the Christian life is only an imitation and expression of the life which Jesus Christ led for us, so the Christian death ought to be only an imitation and expression of the death which Jesus Christ endured for us. Jesus Christ died to satisfy the justice of God for the sins of all men, and to put an end to the reign of iniquity, to render to His Father the most perfect obedience, by submitting to the sentence of death justly pronounced against all sinners, whose place He held, to render by His death an infinite homage to the majesty of God, and to acknowledge His sovereign dominion over all creatures. Every Christian is obliged to accept death in these same dispositions, and should esteem himself only too happy in the thought that Jesus Christ wished to unite the Sacrifice of His divine life, infinitely more precious than the lives of all men and angels, with the sacrifice which each one of us should make to God of our miserable and unworthy life, and that He wished to render our death,

---

4   We have so often met, in the exercise of our holy ministry, with souls who have an excessive fear of death, that we have thought it a duty to add to the consoling reflections of St. Francis de Sales another chapter, the most solid we know on the subject. [This note and this section appear to have been written by Fr. Huguet, the compiler.—*Publisher,* 2013.]

by uniting it with His, capable of meriting for us an eternal life. To die without participating in these dispositions of Jesus Christ at death, is not to die as a Christian, it is to die of necessity as a beast, it is to die as the reprobate.[5]

Every Christian is obliged to labor for the acquisition of these dispositions during his whole life, which is only given him to learn how to die well. We should often adore in Jesus Christ that ardent zeal which He had to satisfy the justice of God and to destroy sin, that spirit of obedience and sacrifice in which He lived and died, and which He still retains in the mystery of the Eucharist. We should ask Him to share it with us, especially during the time of the Holy Sacrifice of the Mass and Communion, when Jesus Christ offers Himself again to His Father in these same dispositions, and comes to us to communicate them to us. The more we participate in these holy dispositions, the less we shall fear a death which ought to be most precious and meritorious before God, and which will be the more so, as we shall more fully enter into the designs of Jesus Christ, who, dying really but once, to render to His Father the supreme honor which was due to Him, desired to offer to Him till the end of ages the death of each of His members, as a continuation of His sacrifice.

One of the chief effects of the Incarnation and death of Jesus Christ has been to deliver us from the fear of death: He became man, and a mortal man, *that He might destroy by His death him who was the prince of death, that is to say, the devil, and that He might deliver those whom the fear of*

---

5 A Christian would implicitly participate in these dispositions simply by being in the state of grace.—*Publisher,* 2013.

death held in continual servitude during life. Is it not in some manner to dishonor the victory of Jesus Christ over death, to tremble before an enemy whom He has vanquished, and to remain still in slavery through fear of dying?

Jesus Christ ardently desired the arrival of the hour that would consummate His sacrifice, by the effusion of His blood: "I have a baptism," so He calls His Passion, "wherewith I am to be baptized, and how am I straitened until it be accomplished!" Should not a Christian, who has the honor of being one of His members, enter into His spirit, and desire the accomplishment of the baptism with which he is to be baptized? For death ought to appear to the true Christian as a baptism, in which he is to be washed from all his sins, and regenerated to a life of immortality, perfectly exempt from every corruption of sin. We should, then, like Jesus, desire with ardor to sacrifice our life as soon as possible: firstly, to render to the sovereign majesty of God, and all His divine perfections, the greatest glory that any creature can render to Him, and to render the most perfect homage to the death of Jesus Christ, our God and Saviour; secondly, to offer to God the most worthy thanksgiving, in gratitude for having sacrificed for us the life of His Son on the cross, as well as for having continued during so many ages to immolate His Body and Blood on our altars, and in gratitude for having given us His Holy Spirit and the life of grace, which is more precious than all the lives in the world; thirdly, to offer to God the fullest satisfaction that we are able to offer Him for our sins, by offering Him our death in union with that of Jesus Christ; fourthly, to draw down upon ourselves the greatest mercies of God, by an humble acceptance of death, and by the continual sacrifice which we shall make to Him of our life. For, although our life is so vile a thing, so little worthy of being offered to God in sacrifice, defiled as it is with so many sins, yet it is the most considerable present we can make to Him; and God is so good as to receive this remnant of sin, as a sacrifice of sweet odor.

A countless number of martyrs, of every age, sex, and country, have run to death with joy, and looked upon it as their greatest happiness to be able to sacrifice themselves for God in the midst of the most dreadful torments. The pagan or irregular life which some among them had led previously did not stay their ardor; because they hoped by their death entirely to repair the past. "Why," says St. Jerome, "do we not imitate them in something?" Are we not, like them, the disciples of a God crucified for our salvation, and destined to the same kingdom of Heaven? It is true that we have not, like them, the happiness of offering to God a bloody death; but, why should we not endeavor to supply its place, by the continual oblation that we can make to Him of the kind of death which He destines for us? "For I venture to say," adds this holy father, "that there is as much, and perhaps more, merit in offering to Him our life during the successive moments in which He preserves it to us, than in losing it once by the cruelty of executioners. The sacrifice which we make to God of our life, if sincere, is the greatest act of love that we can make." St. Augustine says: "If the angels could envy any privilege in man, it is his ability to die for the love of God."

We ask of God every day that His kingdom should

come. This kingdom of God will be perfectly established in us only by death, which will be for each of us an end to sin, the destruction of concupiscence, and the beginning of the absolute reign of justice and charity. To ask of God, every day, the coming of His kingdom, and, at the same time, to fear death excessively—are these things easily allied? The desire of the kingdom of God and of eternal life is essential to salvation. "It is not sufficient," says St. Augustine, "to believe by faith in a blessed life, we must love it by charity, and wish that we were already in the celestial abode; and it is impossible to have these dispositions in the heart, without being glad to depart from this life." At the commencement of the divine prayer in which we ask of God the coming of His kingdom, He orders us to say to Him: *Our Father, Who art in Heaven.* If we sincerely believe that God is our Father, and we His children, how can we fear to go to our Heavenly Father, in order to reign with Him, to enjoy His possessions, and to repose forever on His bosom?

The Scripture represents all the faithful as so many persons who expect the last coming of Jesus Christ, who love His coming, and who go forward to meet Him as far as lies in them by their groans and desires. Why are we Christians? Why are we converted to God? "It is," says St. Paul, "to serve the true and living God, and to expect the Heaven of His Son Jesus, whom He has raised up, and who has delivered us from the wrath to come." To whom will the Lord, *as a just judge, render the crown of justice on the great day?* The same Apostle answers, that it will be *to those who love His coming. Since the earth, and all that it contains, must be consumed by fire,* which will precede the coming of the great Judge, "What ought you to be," says St. Peter to all the faithful, "and what ought to be the sanctity of your life, the piety of your actions, awaiting, and, as it were, hastening by your desires, the coming of the day of the Lord?" Jesus Christ, after having given a description of the frightful signs which will precede His coming, after having told us that men will wither away for fear in expectation of the evils with which the world of the impious will be threatened, addresses immediately to all His disciples who were present, and to all those who should follow Him during the course of ages, these sweet words of consolation and joy: "As for you, when these things begin to happen, look up, and lift up your heads, because your redemption is at hand. . . . When you shall see these things come to pass, know that the kingdom of God is nigh." The great maxims which the Apostles and Jesus Christ Himself teach us, accord perfectly with an ardent desire of death; but do they accord with an excessive fear of death? Are we not afraid to dishonor those great truths, by the opposition that we show between the dispositions which they require, and those which we entertain? "Jesus Christ," says St. Augustine, "will share His kingdom with all those who shall have sincerely desired that His kingdom should come." "He will render," says the Apostle, "the crown of justice to those who love His coming." What, then, should we desire more than His arrival, since it is the sure means of our reigning with Him?

Many persons are tormented at death with the remembrance of their crimes, and, seeing that they have done no penance, they are tempted to despair. "Oh, if I had fasted! Oh, if I had performed great charities for the poor! Alas! I am no longer in a state to perform them. What will become of me? What shall I do?" You can do something greater than all you have mentioned, namely, accept death, and unite it with that of Jesus Christ. There is no mortification comparable to this: it is the deepest humiliation, the greatest impoverishment, the most terrible penance; and I do not at all doubt but that he who is grieved for having offended God, and who accepts death willingly in satisfaction for his sins, will immediately obtain pardon. What a consolation to be able to perform while dying a greater penance than all the anchorets have been able to perform in deserts, and this at a time when one would seem no longer able to do anything! What a pity to see an innumerable multitude of persons deprive themselves of the fruit of death, which of all the pains of life is the one of most merit! *Ut quid perditio haec?*[6] Why waste so advantageous an occasion of honoring God, satisfying His justice, discharging one's debts, and purchasing Heaven?

I acknowledge that your life is nothing in comparison with that of Our Lord Jesus Christ; but, when offered through love, it is of inestimable value. What does God care about an alms of two farthings? Yet the poor widow, in the Gospel, who gave it, deserved to be praised by the Son of God, and to be preferred to the Scribes and Pharisees, who had given much more considerable alms, because, says He, she has given all that she had, and, notwithstanding her poverty, has given it with a great heart. *Haec de penuria*

---

6   "To what purpose is this waste?" (*Matt.* 26:8).—*Publisher, 2013.*

sua omnia quae habuit misit totum victum suum.[7]

We can say the same of him who gives his life to God: he gives all that he has, without reserving anything, and this is what renders death precious. This is what made the early Christians run with so much eagerness to martyrdom: they all wished to give back to Our Lord the life which they had received from Him, and to compensate by their death for that which He had endured for love of them.

We can no longer be martyrs; oh, what an affliction! but still we can die for Jesus Christ! We have a life that we can lose for His love! Oh, what a consolation!

The line of distinction which St. Augustine draws between the perfect and the imperfect is that the perfect suffer life with pain and receive death with joy, while the imperfect receive death only with patience, struggling against themselves to submit to the will of God: preferring however to yield to what He requires of them, arming themselves with courage to overcome the desire of life, and to receive death with submission and peace.

Perfection, therefore, consists in desiring to die, that we may no longer be imperfect, that we may wholly cease to offend God, that God may reign perfectly in us, and that this body of sin, which we carry about with us until death, may, in punishment of its continual revolts against God, be reduced to dust, fully to satisfy His justice and sanctity, and, by this last and most profound humiliation, fully to repair all the injuries which it has committed against the Divine Majesty. We rise towards perfection in proportion as these

---

7 "She of her want cast in all she had, even her whole living." (Cf. *Mark* 12:44). —*Publisher,* 2013.

holy desires of death become more ardent and sincere, and the quickest means of becoming perfect is to desire death with one's whole heart.

The preparations that we might wish to bring with us to our last sacrifice ought not, when the hour of consummating it arrives, to lead us to desire that the sacrifice should be deferred. These preparations are less necessary than submission to the will of God. Our submission can supply the place of these preparations, but nothing can supply the want of our submission; a thing which souls, even the most imperfect, should never forget. It is more advantageous for us to appear before Jesus Christ, when He announces His coming, than to expose ourselves to the risk of meeting Him too late, by expecting that we shall afterwards be better prepared. The essential preparation is to go before Him with confidence and love; and we must think only of exciting acts of these virtues. It ought to be a great subject of humiliation and confusion to us, not to feel a holy ardor and impatience to go to Him. Happy are we, says St. Chrysostom, if we sigh and groan continually within ourselves, awaiting the accomplishment of our divine adoption, which will be the redemption and deliverance of our bodies and souls—if we desire to depart from this world with as much ardor and impatience as the banished desire an end of their exile, and captives of their imprisonment.[8] This impatience, adds the holy doctor, which we testify to God, will serve much to obtain the pardon of our sins, and will be the best of all dispositions for appearing before Him.

---

8   Chrys., *Hom. xvii in Gen. et alib.*

We have elsewhere shown that no person, however holy his life may have been, should rely upon his virtues, if God should examine them without mercy. It is to be already condemned, to consent to be judged without a great mercy. Confidence in the divine mercy, and in the merits of Jesus Christ, is the only security for all. Since, then, we must always return to this point, let us, from this moment, abandon ourselves to these dispositions in life and in death. Let us hold, as a certain truth, that the more fully we thus abandon ourselves, the more just shall we be, and the more agreeable our sacrifices to God.